Fearon's

MW01491069

Refrigerator Display Rewards

Reproducible Activities
for
Show 'n Tell at Home

Fearon Teacher Aids
Carthage, Illinois

Illustrated by Marilynn Barr

ISBN 0-8224-3152-1

Printed in the United States of America

1. 9 8 7 6 5 4 3

Contents

Introduction

This set of reproducible materials is designed to be used in pre-k and kindergarten early learning programs. Each reward activity features the child's art work, printing, cutting, coloring, and or pasting. The reward should serve as a culminating activity for a developmental learning sequence. Parents should be encouraged to post the child's work and listen to the child demonstrate the skill represented by the reward activity sheet.

Most activity sheets are self-explanatory. Some require simple materials and teacher preparation. There are complete directions for using the activity sheets in the following section (pages 5–8). Always fill in your name and the date and help the child print his or her name (if necessary) before sending the work home. A note to parents at the bottom of each reward may be cut off before duplicating (without spoiling the reward) if you wish to write your own note.

The reproducible letter to parents on page 9 may be copied as written or used as a springboard for creating your own letter that introduces parents to the rewards.

While presented in a typical developmental sequence, these skills will be mastered by different children at different times during the year. The skills are those found in most early learning programs. Most activities include a variety of skills—cutting, pasting, coloring, following directions, spatial concepts, and manipulation of parts.

Directions for Using the Activities

I Can Lace and Tie, pages 11 and 12

Reproduce the reward page and the shoe pattern on heavy paper. Cut out the shoe and punch holes for the laces and for the attachment tie at the top of the shoe. Let each child color the shoe and thread yarn or cord through the lacing holes. Punch holes in the reward page as noted. Using yarn or cord, help each child attach the shoe to the reward page and tie a bow. Fill in your name and the date. Help the child print his or her name on the line before sending home.

I Know When to Cross, page 13

Reproduce the reward page. Let each child color the pedestrian signals. You may want to help the children color the signals according to signage in your area.

My Traffic Light, page 14

Reproduce the reward page. Help each child color the signal appropriately. It is not as important for the children to recognize the color words, as it is that they recognize the position of the colors and what the colors mean with safety words.

I Can Tell Left and Right, page 15

Reproduce a reward sheet for each child. Let the child make the appropriate handprint in the space. Use any color of dry tempera paint mixed with small amounts of liquid detergent and liquid starch to make the printing mixture. Pour a thin layer of this mixture into a shallow pan. Have newsprint ready for practice prints. Help each child make his or her best prints. If you wish, children may make hand tracings with crayons instead of tempera paint prints.

I Can Name These Colors, page 16

Reproduce a copy of the reward for each child who recognizes the color words. Let the child color the circles the correct color and practice naming the colors.

I Can Say My Telephone Number, page 17

Reproduce the telephone number reward for each child. Let the child color the picture. The child may choose to use a special color, such as red, for those numbers on the keypad that make up his or her telephone number. Help each child print the telephone number on the lines, including the area code. Children may want to practice touching their telephone numbers on the keypads.

I Know These Shapes, page 18

Reproduce the reward for each child. Help the child practice the shape words and trace each shape with crayons. Children may wish to add more shapes to the page.

I Can Cut and Paste Squares, page 19
I Can Cut and Paste Triangles, page 20
I Can Cut and Paste Circles, page 21

For each of these activities, reproduce the reward page for each child. Let the children color the shapes at the bottom of the page, and then cut and paste them to fit in the shapes inside the border. Let the children cut out items from magazines that are correct shape and then paste them inside the border. Help the children trim the bottom edges of their rewards neatly.

I Can Cut and Paste Shapes, page 22

Reproduce the reward page for each child. Ask the children to color the shapes according to the color code. Show the children how to cut the shapes from the bottom of the sheet and paste them to match on the reward sheet. Help the children trim the bottom edges of their rewards neatly.

I Can Make a Puzzle, page 23

Reproduce the reward page for each child. Ask the children to color the picture at the bottom of the page. Help them cut the picture apart on the dotted lines and reassemble inside the border under the title. Let them paste it in place. Help the children trim the bottom edges of their rewards neatly.

I Can Count to Five, page 24

Reproduce the reward page and let the children connect the dots to complete the picture and then use crayons to color their work.

I Can Make Jack-O'-Lanterns, page 25

Reproduce the reward page for each child. Help the children draw and color the correct number of Jack-O'-Lanterns next to the numerals.

I Can Tell About Fall, page 26

Reproduce the reward page for each child. Ask the children to color the pictures in the boxes. Talk with them about the signs of fall—leaves turn bright colors and flutter from the trees; squirrels gather nuts for the winter; the air is cooler so girls and boys need sweaters and jackets to keep warm. Help the children cut and paste the small pictures into the correct boxes on the activity sheet.

I Can Tell About Me, page 27

Reproduce the reward page for each child. Print each child's name on the line. Let the children draw and color pictures of their homes and themselves in the appropriate spaces. Let them take turns telling the group about their pictures before sending the pages home.

I Can Say My Address, page 28

Reproduce the reward page for each child. Print each child's name and address on the primary ruled lines on the mail box. Use a black permanent marker for the printing so the children may color the picture without smearing the printing. Let the children practice repeating their addresses to the group before sending the pages home.

I Can Make Thanksgiving Dinner, page 29

Reproduce the reward page for each child. Ask the children to color all the pictures at the bottom of the page. Then let them choose the foods they wish to eat for their holiday meals and paste the pictures of these foods on the table. Help the children trim the bottom edges of their rewards neatly.

I Can Print These Numerals, page 30

Reproduce the reward page for each child. Ask the children to color and count the bears. Ask them to trace the numerals with crayons.

I Know About Winter, page 31
Reproduce the reward page for each child. Talk about the changes in the weather—temperature, clouds, rain, ice, and snow. Let the children color the pictures at the bottom of the page. Ask them to paste only the winter pictures inside the border. Tell them to paste the other pictures on the backs of their papers.

I Know Which Is Big, page 32
Reproduce the reward page for each child. Let the children color the pictures. Ask the children to look at each set of objects and to choose the bigger one of the group and circle it.

I Can Tell About Birds, page 33
Reproduce the reward page for each child. Let the children color the pictures and talk about their meanings. Ask them to draw other pictures to illustrate the sentences.

I Can Tell About Mammals, page 34
Reproduce the reward page for each child. Let the children color the pictures. Ask them to draw lines to match the baby animals with their mothers.

I Can Tell About Fish, page 35
Reproduce the reward page for each child. Let the children color the pictures. Ask them to draw other pictures to illustrate the sentences.

I Can Tell About Community Helpers, page 36
Reproduce the reward page for each child. Let the children color the pictures. Help them cut out the pictures and paste them correctly inside the borders. Help the children trim the bottom edges of their rewards neatly.

This Is My Farm, page 37
Reproduce the reward page for each child. For each child, have 4 or 5 small sized cotton balls for the lamb, a jar lid with seeds for planting, a short section of pipe cleaner to paste on the pig for a tail, and a short piece of string for the horse's rope. Let the children color the pictures. Give each one a small amount of paste and the collage materials. Help them paste the cotton balls on the lamb's body, the seeds in the garden, and the rope on the horse's halter. Show them how to twist the pipe cleaner to make a pig's tail and paste it in place on the pig.

My Valentine Colors, page 38
Reproduce the reward page for each child. Give each child small containers of red, white, and yellow tempera paints and a brush. Each child will also need a container of water and a paper towel or old cloth for wiping brushes. Show the children how to mix the colors to create pinks and oranges. Show them how to rinse and dry the brush to avoid mixing unwanted colors. Let the children practice mixing colors on scrap pieces of paper before working on the reward pages. Listen to them name the colors they have painted.

I Know About St. Patrick's Day, page 39
Reproduce the reward page for each child. Follow the procedures used for "My Valentine Colors" above. Change the paint colors to yellow and blue.

I Can Say My ABC's, page 40

Reproduce the reward page for each child. Help the children complete the picture by following the dots from A to Z. Let them color their pictures.

I Know About Plants, page 41

Reproduce the reward page for each child. Let the children color the plants. Help them color and cut out the pictures at the bottom of the page. Show them how to paste the pictures in the boxes to give their plants light and water.

I Know About the Parts of Plants, pages 42 and 43

Reproduce page 42 on white paper and page 43 on green paper (1/2 of page 43 for each child). Give each child several short pieces of string or yarn for the plants' roots. Let the children color the reward page. Help them cut out the green stems and leaves and paste them in place. Show them how to paste the strings to create a root system for the plants.

I Know How Plants Grow, page 44

Reproduce the reward page for each child. Before sending this activity home, your students should have had the opportunity to plant a seed in a paper cup, water it, and observe its growth. Let the children color the pictures on the reward page and take turns telling the group about their plants' progress.

I Know About Springtime, page 45

Reproduce the reward page for each child. Let the children cut pictures from old magazines, greeting cards, or catalogs that show plants blooming, new-born farm animals, sunshine, trees with new leaves, and the like. Let them paste their pictures to illustrate the processes of spring.

My Bird's Nest, page 46

Reproduce the reward page for each child. Cut newspaper or scrap paper into thin, short strips so that each child can have enough to build a nest. Ask the children to color the baby birds, and the parent bird at the bottom of the page. Help them cut out the birds. Show them how to color the tree branch and then paste strips of paper to create a nest. Help them paste the baby birds in the nest and the parent on the tree branch. Help the children trim the bottom edges of their pages neatly.

I Can Count to Ten, page 47

Reproduce the reward page for each child. Let the children complete the dot to dot and then color the pictures.

I Can Tell About My Picture, page 48

Reproduce the reward page for each child. Ask the children to draw pictures that tell a story. Listen to their stories, and on the lines, write a few sentences that they have dictated.

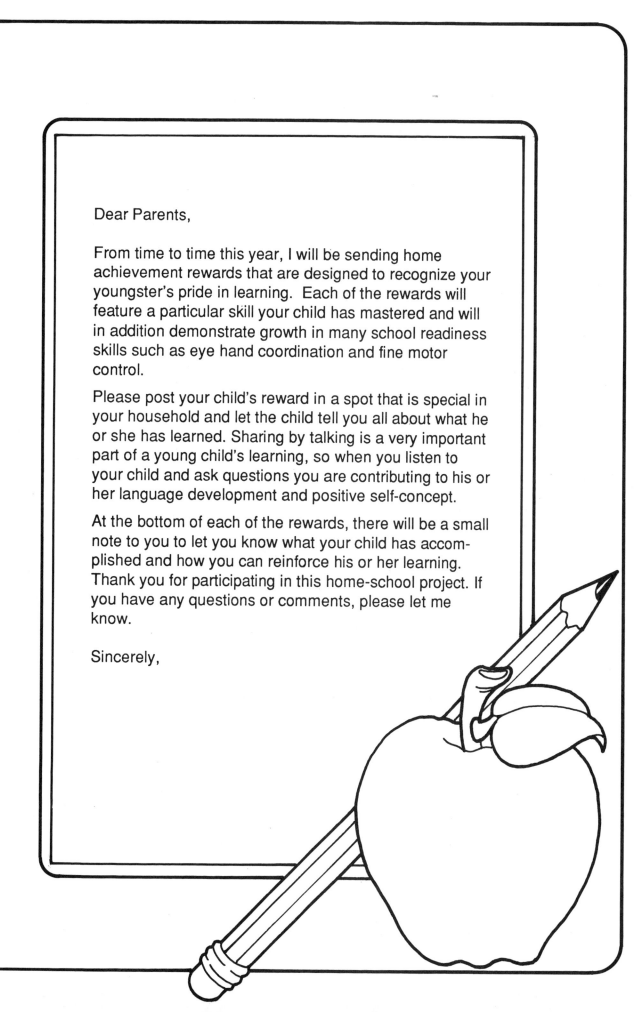

Dear Parents,

From time to time this year, I will be sending home achievement rewards that are designed to recognize your youngster's pride in learning. Each of the rewards will feature a particular skill your child has mastered and will in addition demonstrate growth in many school readiness skills such as eye hand coordination and fine motor control.

Please post your child's reward in a spot that is special in your household and let the child tell you all about what he or she has learned. Sharing by talking is a very important part of a young child's learning, so when you listen to your child and ask questions you are contributing to his or her language development and positive self-concept.

At the bottom of each of the rewards, there will be a small note to you to let you know what your child has accomplished and how you can reinforce his or her learning. Thank you for participating in this home-school project. If you have any questions or comments, please let me know.

Sincerely,

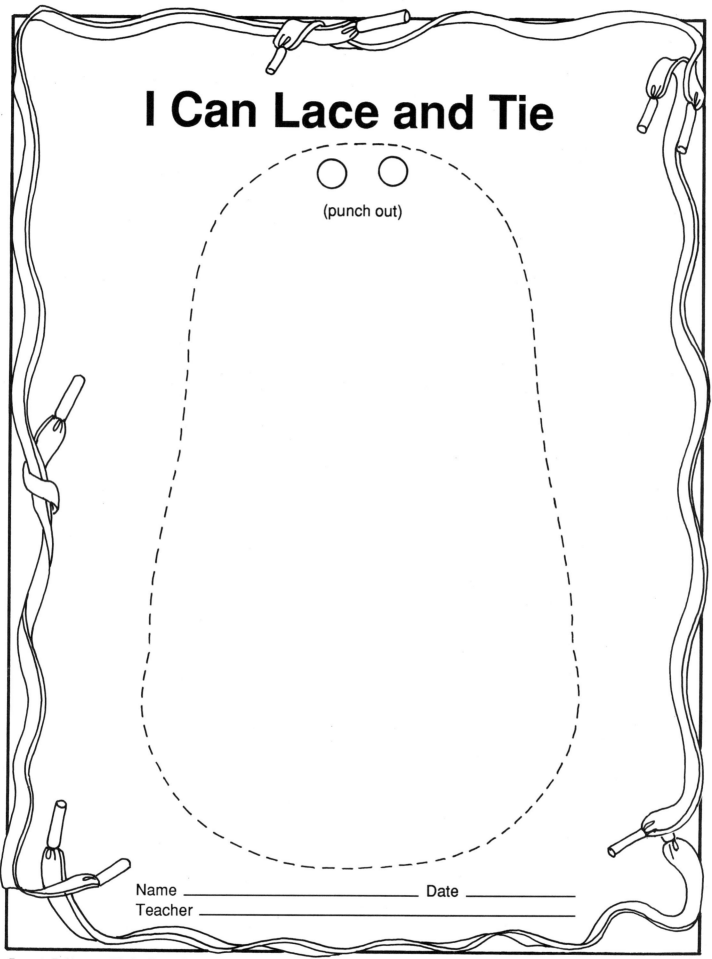

I Can Lace and Tie

(punch out)

Name _____ Date _____

Teacher _____

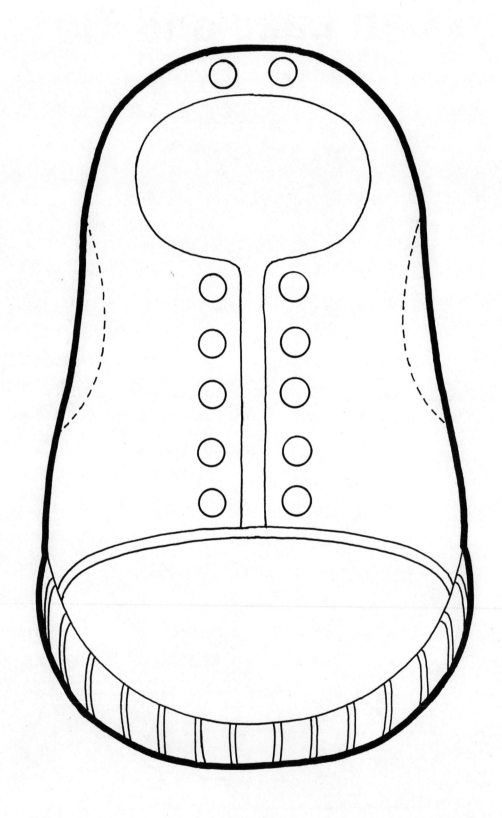

I Know When to Cross

This Means
Wait

This means
Walk

Name_____ Date_____
Teacher_____

My Traffic Light

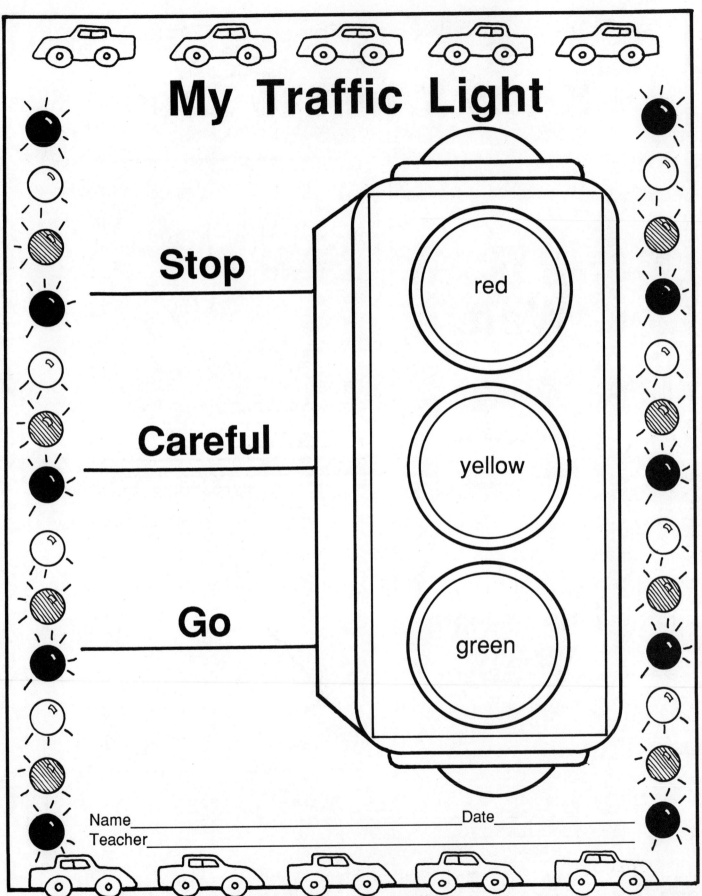

Stop — red

Careful — yellow

Go — green

Name_____ Date_____
Teacher_____

Your child recognizes the position, color, and meaning of the traffic signal. Let your child tell you the meaning of each signal.

I Can Tell Left and Right

My left hand   My right hand

Name_____Date_____
Teacher_____

Your child has made these handprints and can easily distinguish left and right.

Fearon's Refrigerator Display Rewards © 1989

I Can Name These Colors

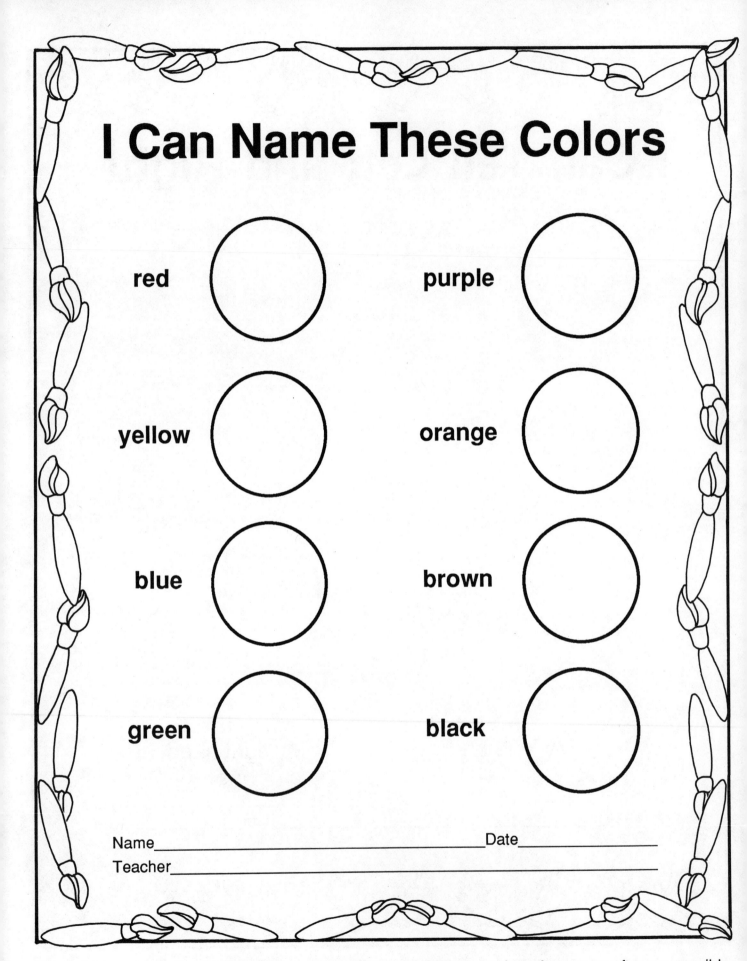

red

purple

yellow

orange

blue

brown

green

black

Name_____ Date_____

Teacher_____

Your child can say the names of these colors. Let your child name them for you as often as possible.

Fearon's Refrigerator Display Rewards © 1989

I Can Say My Telephone Number

Name_____ Date_____
Teacher_____

Your child can say his or her telephone number. Let your child tell you the number and practice by touching the numbers on the number pad.

Fearon's Refrigerator Display Rewards © 1989

I Know These Shapes

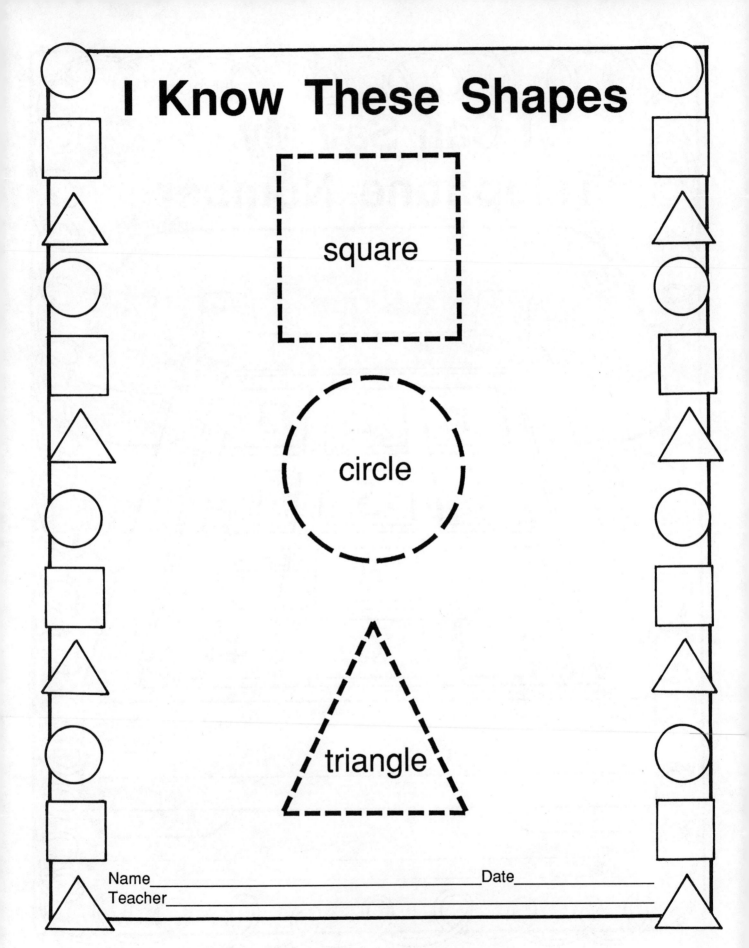

square

circle

triangle

Name_____Date_____
Teacher_____

Your child knows the names of these shapes and has traced them.

Fearon's Refrigerator Display Rewards © 1989

I Can Cut and Paste Squares

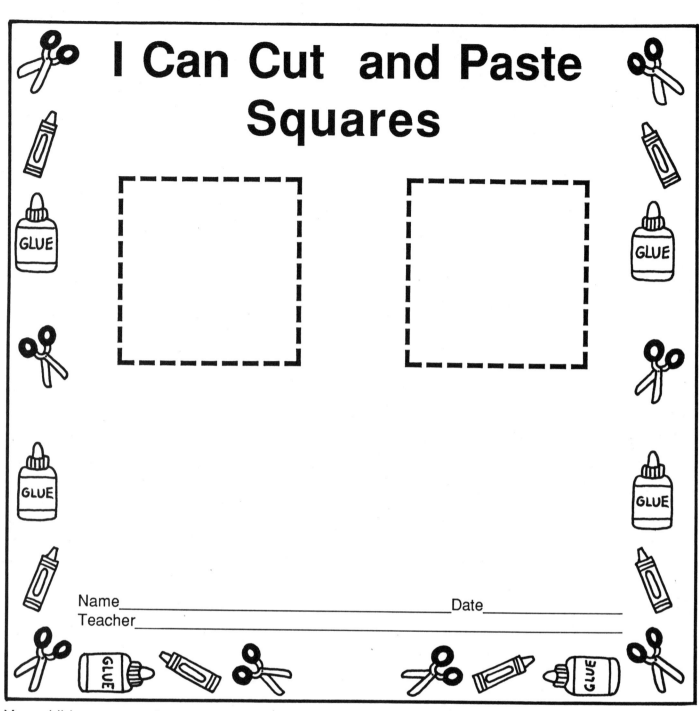

Name_____Date_____
Teacher_____

Your child can recognize a square and use his or her scissors to cut neatly.

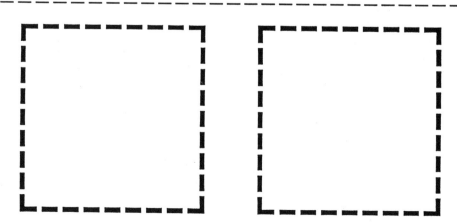

I Can Cut and Paste Triangles

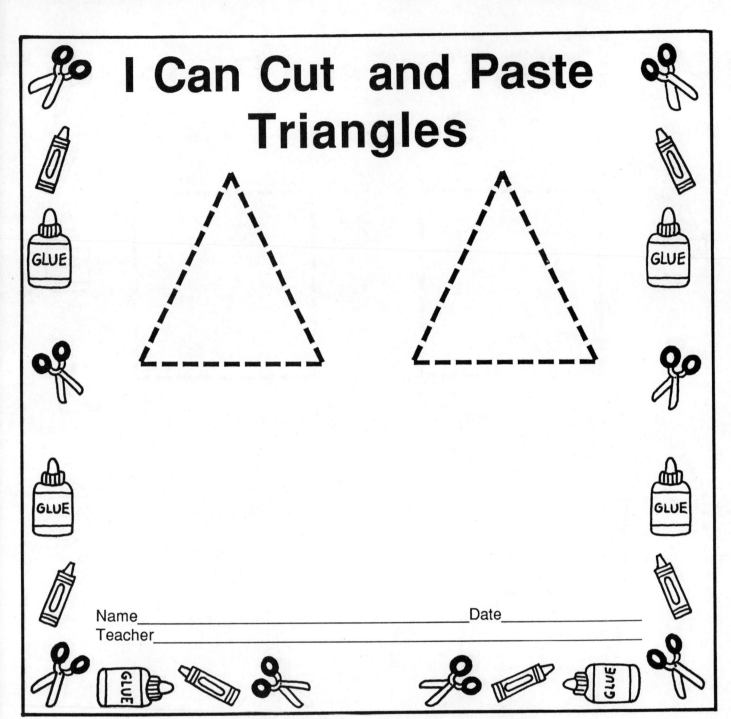

Name_____Date_____
Teacher_____

Your child can recognize a triangle and use his or her scissors to cut neatly.

- -

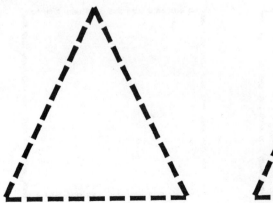

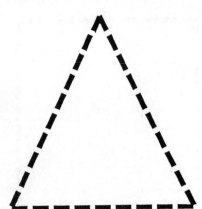

I Can Cut and Paste
Circles

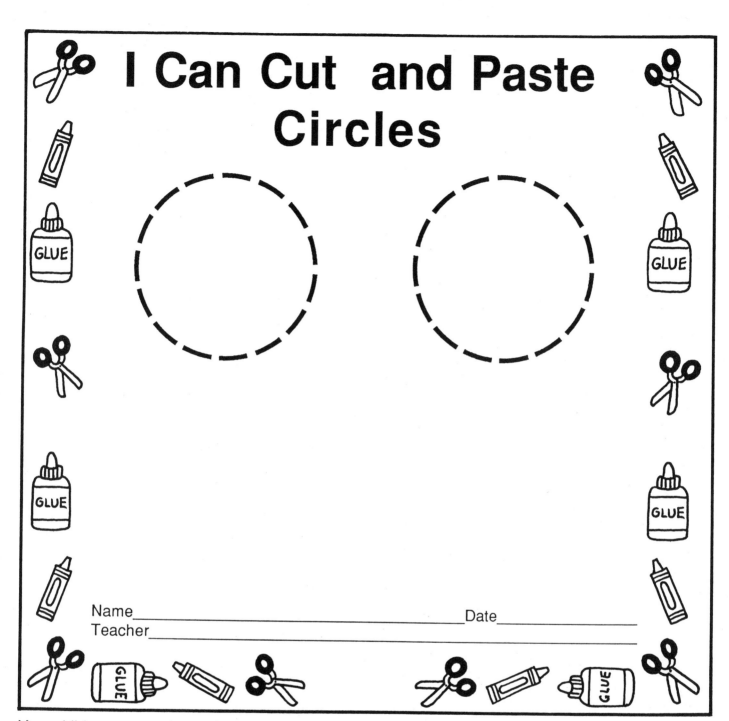

Name_____Date_____
Teacher_____

Your child can recognize a circle and use his or her scissors to cut neatly.

- -

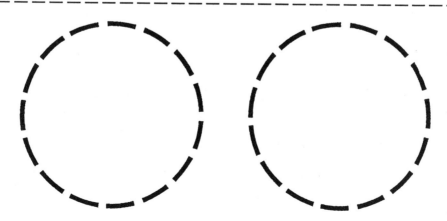

I Can Cut and Paste Shapes

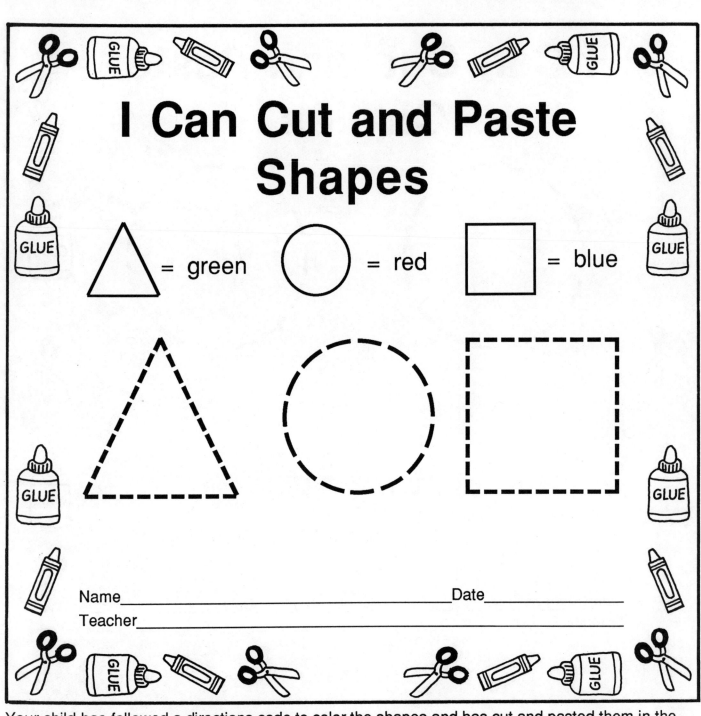

△ = green ○ = red ☐ = blue

Name_____Date_____

Teacher_____

Your child has followed a directions code to color the shapes and has cut and pasted them in the correct position. This project demonstrates progress in cutting, coloring, pasting, and following directions.

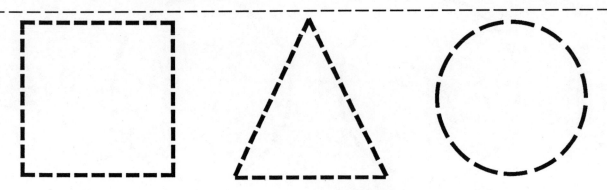

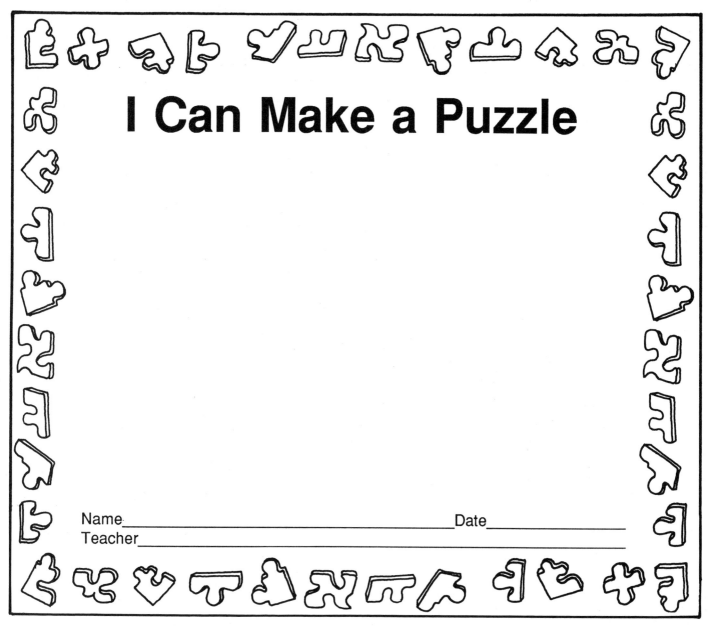

I Can Make a Puzzle

Name_____ Date_____
Teacher_____

Your child has colored, cut out, and pasted the pieces to create a picture puzzle. This project demonstrates your child's progress in cutting, coloring, pasting, recognizing parts of a whole, and following directions.

I Can Count to Five

Name_____ Date_____
Teacher_____

Your child can recognize the order of numerals to five. This dot-to-dot picture demonstrates counting and small motor skills development.

Fearon's Refrigerator Display Rewards © 1989

I Can Make
Jack-O'-Lanterns

1 _____

2 _____

3 _____

4 _____

5 _____

Name_____ Date_____

Teacher_____

Your child recognizes the concept of number and can create sets to illustrate this understanding.

Fearon's Refrigerator Display Rewards © 1989

I Can Tell About Fall

Name_____ Date_____

Teacher_____

Your child understands the changes that take place during the fall season.

Fearon's Refrigerator Display Rewards © 1989

I Can Tell About Me

This is my name. _____

This is my home.

This is me.

Teacher _____   Date _____

Your child can recognize his or her printed name. Please allow your child to tell you about the drawings and point out his or her name.

I Can Say My Address

Teacher_____ Date_____

Your child can say his or her address. This is an important safety measure. Let your child practice saying your address and tell you about the things that might be in the mailbox.

Fearon's Refrigerator Display Rewards © 1989

I Can Make Thanksgiving Dinner

Name_____ Date_____

Teacher_____

Your child has colored, cut, and pasted the Thanksgiving foods picture. He or she has learned about holiday traditions, and with this project demonstrates progress in small motor skills. Please let your child tell you about Thanksgiving.

I Can Print These Numerals

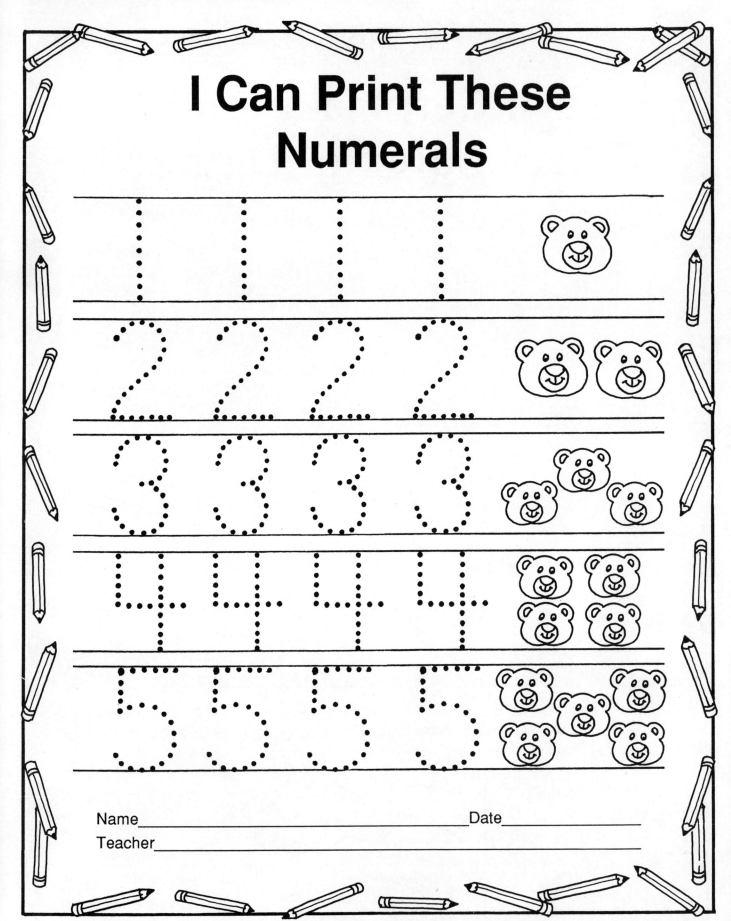

Name_____ Date_____

Teacher_____

Your child has colored these pictures and traced the numerals to demonstrate an understanding of the formation of the numerals as well as the concept of number.

I Know About Winter

Name_____Date_____

Teacher_____

Your child has learned about the winter season. Please let your child tell you about how the weather changes and how animals and people make changes too.

I Know Which Is Big

Name_____Date_____
Teacher_____

Your child understands the concepts "big" and "small" and can visually pick out the bigger of two or three items. Please let your child demonstrate this ability to you by using objects around your house.

Fearon's Refrigerator Display Rewards © 1989

I Can Tell About Birds

Birds lay eggs.

Birds have feathers.

Most birds can fly.

Name_____Date_____
Teacher_____

Your child can recognize the characteristics of birds. The drawings he or she has made demonstrate fine motor skills development as well.

I Can Tell About Mammals

Mammals have babies.

mothers   babies

Name_____ Date_____

Teacher_____

Your child understands that mammals give birth to live young. He or she can match a parent animal to its offspring.

I Can Tell About Fish

Fish swim in water.

Fish have scales.

Fish lay eggs.

Name_____Date_____
Teacher_____

Your child can recognize the characteristics of fish. The drawings he or she has made demonstrate fine motor skills development as well.

I Can Tell About Community Helpers

Name_____   Date_____
Teacher_____

Your child can recognize the work done by community helpers and can match pictures of these people with their activities or tools.

Fearon's Refrigerator Display Rewards © 1989

This Is My Farm

Name_____ Date_____

Teacher_____

Your child has learned about farms and farm animals. Please allow your child to tell you about his or her farm.

My Valentine Colors

Name_____Date_____
Teacher_____

Your child is learning about mixing paints. He or she has mixed the colors for the Valentine project here. Please let him or her tell you about the colors. Happy Valentine's Day!

I Know About St. Patrick's Day

Name_____ Date_____

Teacher_____

Your child has mixed the colors for this project. Please let your child find items in your home that are the same colors.

I Can Say My ABC's

Name_____ Date_____
Teacher_____

Your child can say the alphabet in order and recognize the letters. This project also shows progress in eye hand coordination and following directions.

I Know About Plants

Name_____ Date_____
Teacher_____

Your child understands that plants need water, soil, and light to grow.

I Know About the Parts of Plants

Name_____ Date_____
Teacher_____

Your child has created a collage plant and understands the parts of a typical plant—roots, stem, and leaves. Please let your child tell you about plants.

          Fearon's Refrigerator Display Rewards © 1989

I Know About the Parts of Plants, part 2

I Know About the Parts of Plants, part 2

I Know How Plants Grow

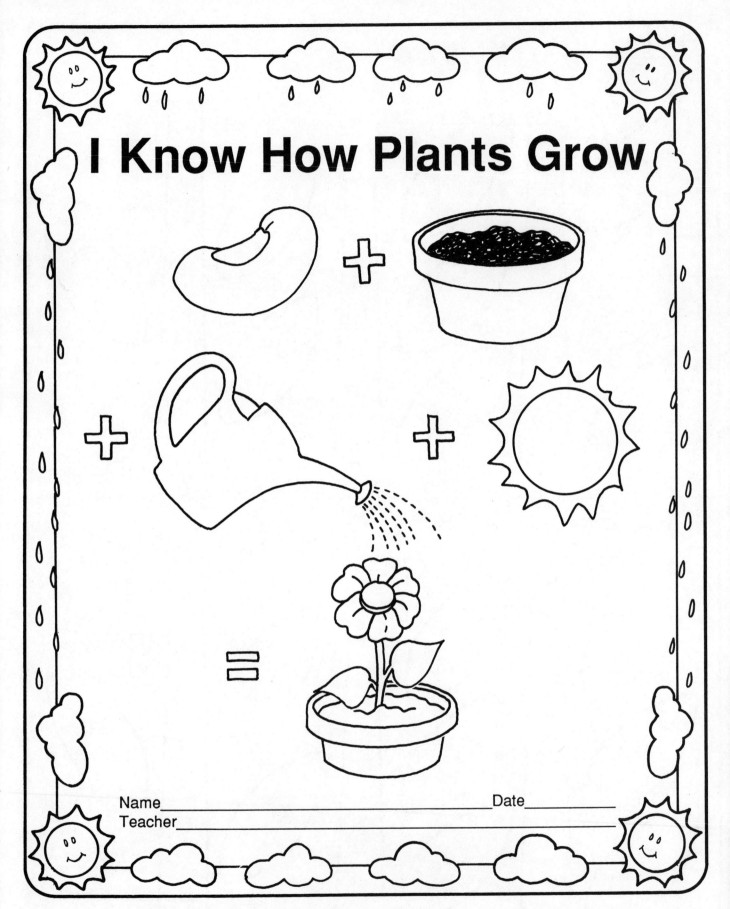

Name_____ Date_____
Teacher_____

Your child has planted a real seed and has seen a plant develop from it. Let your child tell you about his or her plant.

 Fearon's Refrigerator Display Rewards © 1989

I Know About Springtime

Name_____Date_____
Teacher_____

Your child has learned about the changes that occur in the spring. He or she has made this picture to help tell about spring.

Fearon's Refrigerator Display Rewards © 1989

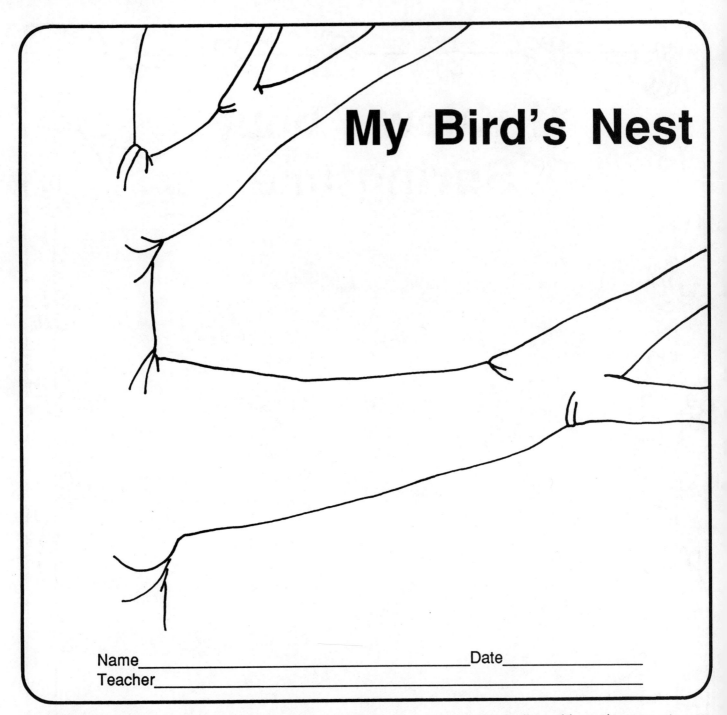

My Bird's Nest

Name_____ Date_____
Teacher_____

Your child has learned about birds' nesting behavior—how the nest is built and how the parents care for the eggs and the young birds. Please let your child tell you about his or her bird's nest.

I Can Count to Ten

Name_____Date_____

Teacher_____

Your child can count and recognize numerals to ten. This project also shows growth in fine motor skills development.

Fearon's Refrigerator Display Rewards © 1989

I Can Tell About My Picture

Your child's drawing illustrates a story that he or she can tell. Please let your child share this story with you.

Fearon's Refrigerator Display Rewards © 1989